Face to Face with Love

Anthony Cabalar

Copyright © 2021 Anthony Cabalar

All rights reserved.

ISBN:9798735830627

DEDICATION

Dedicated to Jesus

FACE TO FACE WITH LOVE

CONTENTS

	Acknowledgments	i
1	Introduction	1
2	You Can See God	Pg 6
3	The Encounter	Pg 23
4	Desire and Your Heart	Pg 31
5	Imagination	Pg 44
6	Veil: Body, Soul, and Spirit	Pg 55
7	YOU ARE A SON	Pg 74
8	Testimonies	Pg 80
9	Final Thoughts	Pg 98

Introduction

Very rarely will anyone die for a righteous person, though for a good person someone might possibly dare to die. But God demonstrates his own love for us in this: While we were still sinners, Christ died for us.
Romans 5:7-8 NIV

Before we begin, I'd like to express a truth that we all must be reminded of on a regular basis: You are loved by Jesus.

Think about that right now. Sit back, relax, and ponder, "Jesus loves me. He really loves me."

The love of God is such a huge thing to grasp. God Himself, the creator of all things seen and unseen, stripped Himself of His power, became a man, took all the wickedness of the world upon Himself, and destroyed it on the cross just for you. You are that special and He would literally do it again just for you. He loves you that much.

The purpose of this book is to help you grow in your relationship with God and to bring you face to face with

Love, the One who loves you more than life itself. The One who loves you more than anything, and who loves you more than anyone.

Jesus has made it possible for you to meet with Him face to face. Jesus, the second Adam, destroyed the curse of the first Adam, brought you back to the Garden to be with Him, made you one with Himself, and deposited all of heaven inside of you. He gave you power and authority when you made Him your Lord and Savior, so you can do all things through Him.

Do you ever ask yourself what life was like in the Garden of Eden? What kind of activities did Adam and Eve do there? I believe these questions are important, for they will help us to realize why we were created.

Take a moment to imagine what Adam and Eve did in the Garden and what the Father created them for. Did they explore and enjoy God's creation and His presence as they walked with Him in the cool of the day? Did they skip stones with Him in the river Pishon or white water raft the four river heads flowing from His throne?

Let's also take a moment to think about why we call God our Father. Is it because He is actually our dad? If He is actually our dad, then did He create us to be a part of His household? If we are part of His household, are we His beneficiaries, like we would be with our earthly parents?

I present these questions about what Adam and Eve did in the Garden before the fall because Jesus has redeemed us to that unblemished state of being through His sacrifice on the cross. We can once again enjoy fellowship with Jesus in the earth as well as in heaven. As we ponder what Adam and Eve did in the Garden and what kind of things they did with Jesus it will help open our minds to the different encounters we can have with Father God, Jesus, and the Holy Spirit.

YOU CAN SEE GOD

He is the image of the invisible God, the firstborn over all creation.
Colossians 1:15 NKJV

And He is the radiance of His glory and the exact representation of His nature, and upholds all things by the word of His power. When He had made purification of sins, He sat down at the right hand of the Majesty on high.
Hebrews 1:3 NASB

Before naptime and bedtime my children and I have a ritual where I tell them a story and then we hang out with Jesus. We individually stand before Jesus and ask Him to take us somewhere. I explained to my children that we can go anywhere with Jesus because there is no limitation with Him. This includes going into the past, future, a cartoon, a picture, and even someone's boogers. They thought that was hilarious.

One night my oldest son said he was going into the future and my second oldest said he was going into my blood. After they closed their eyes for a few minutes, my oldest told me that Jesus showed him that he would be drawing and playing with legos tomorrow morning. My second oldest said that he went into my blood and said it looked like blood.

When morning came around, my oldest drew some pictures and then played with legos. While he was playing with his legos he looked up at me and said, "I guess I was right."

Before I asked Jesus to show me anything that night, I sat back and considered where I should ask Jesus to take me. I have a desire to know the deep things of God. One thing I was curious about was what came before creation. What did God do and what did He look like before He created mankind? How did Yehova (the uncreated one) come into being? I asked Jesus to take me to the time when He created Himself into an image, or became a man Himself.

Then God took me.

I was in a place that looked pitch black. I felt an incredible energy that was God and I saw His thoughts. I felt His love and desire to have a relationship with me. What He showed me was that when He was thinking of coming to earth in human form as Jesus, He recognized how He'd be able to hang out with me if He created Himself into an image. He wanted someone to share His love and creation with. He wanted someone that could be like Him and who He could relate to.

God continued to show me that for Him to be able to fulfill His desires to interact with us as a father does with a child, and be able to share all that He is and has, He had to create Himself into the image of Jesus. And when He would create us, we could be in His image and likeness.

It made me think of these Bible verses:

This is the book of the generations of Adam. In the day when God created man, He made him in the likeness of God. He created them male and female, and He blessed them and named them "mankind" on the day when they were created.
Genesis 5:1-2 NASB

The idea that God made Himself into an image to have a relationship with us and created us to be like Him blew my mind. Besides the verses in the Bible that say we are created in His image and likeness, there is another verse that states that we can do the same works as Jesus. This verse really touches my heart.

> *"Most assuredly, I say to you, he who believes in Me, the works that I do he will do also; and greater works than these he will do, because I go to My Father."*
> **John 14:12 NKJV**

Then He said to me, "If I made Myself into an image to create you, surely I will bless you!"

So what do we have to fear? When we engage our faith and realize God loves us and desires to bless us, we can expect miracles and His blessings each and every day.

To summarize, God created Himself into the image of Jesus so that He could create us in His image, be with us, and engage with us as His family members. That means we can see Him and hang out with Him today.

Some people try to use verses from the Old Testament to say we can't see God, but that's not true. Here is one verse that is commonly used.

But He said, "You cannot see My face; for no man shall see Me, and live."
Exodus 33:20 NKJV

When people use this verse they only reference the middle and last part: "no man shall see Me, and live." If we read the whole chapter of Exodus 33, we will notice Moses had an encounter where he saw God.

Look at what God tells Moses in verse 19.

> Then He said, "I will make all My goodness pass before you, and **I will proclaim the name of the LORD before you**. I will be gracious to whom I will be gracious, and I will have compassion on whom I will have compassion."
> **Exodus 33:19 NKJV (emphasis added)**

What stands out to me in that verse is the part where God distinguishes the image from the uncreated being.

An old Bible scholar once told me that it is very important to take note of the small things mentioned in the Bible. The small things sometimes reveal a larger revelation.

We want to pay attention to when God speaks in the Bible because God always says things for a reason. So why did God say, "I will proclaim the name of the LORD," and not, "I will proclaim My Name"? It wasn't Father God speaking, it was Jesus. Jesus was saying He will proclaim the name of the LORD the name of the GODhead. The LORD translated in Hebrew is Yehovah (Strong's concordance # h3068) or "The existing one."

As we continue reading this passage in Exodus, it says that Moses did see part of God's form.

> *"Then I will take away My hand, and you shall see My back; but My face shall not be seen."*
> **Exodus 33:23 NKJV**

Throughout Exodus and Numbers we witness Moses having numerous encounters with God while he saw God with his eyes. Let's see what God said to Moses' siblings.

> *Miriam and Aaron began to talk against Moses because of his Cushite wife, for he had married a Cushite. "Has the LORD spoken only through Moses?" they asked. "Hasn't he also spoken through us?" And the LORD heard this.*
> *(Now Moses was a very humble man, more humble than anyone else on the face of the earth.)*

At once the LORD said to Moses, Aaron and Miriam, "Come out to the tent of meeting, all three of you." So the three of them went out. Then the LORD came down in a pillar of cloud; he stood at the entrance to the tent and summoned Aaron and Miriam. When the two of them stepped forward, he said, "Listen to my words:
"When there is a prophet among you, I, the LORD, reveal myself to them in visions,
I speak to them in dreams.
But this is not true of my servant Moses;
He is faithful in all my house.
With him I speak face to face, clearly and not in riddles;
He sees the form of the LORD.
Why then were you not afraid to speak against my servant Moses?"

The anger of the LORD burned against them, and he left them.
Numbers 12:1-9 NIV

It is clear in the Old Testament that Moses had a real relationship with Jesus. He was probably one of the closest friends Jesus had in the Old Testament.

Moving forward to the New Testament, do we see people becoming friends with Jesus? Can we also have a real relationship with Jesus? First, let's take a look at why it was so rare for people in the Old Testament to interact with God.

And they heard the voice of the **Lord God walking in the garden** *in the cool of the day: and Adam and his wife hid themselves from the presence of the*

Lord God amongst the trees of the garden.
And the Lord God called unto Adam, and said unto him, Where art thou? And he said, I heard thy voice in the garden, and I was afraid, because I was naked; **and I hid myself.**
Genesis 3:8-10 NKJV (emphasis added)

Adam and Eve fell from their perfect, sinless state in the Garden and because of sin, they could no longer physically interact with God and see His face. In the New Testament God made a way for humanity to return to His original design for us by coming to earth in flesh and blood as Jesus.

Who, being in very nature God, did not consider equality with God something to be used to

his own advantage;
rather, he made himself nothing
by taking the very nature of a servant,
being made in human likeness.
And being found in appearance as a man,
he humbled himself
by becoming obedient to death—
even death on a cross!
Philippians 2:6-8 NIV

Jesus took everyone's sin, past, present, and future, onto Himself when He died on the cross, and therefore destroyed its power. When we receive His free gift of forgiveness for all our sins, we are restored back into relationship with Father God and we can see His face, touch Him, and hear His voice.

That which was from the beginning, which we have heard, which we have seen with our eyes, which we have looked upon, and our hands have handled, concerning the Word of life—
1 John 1:1 NKJV

While he was at the table with them, he took bread, gave thanks, broke it and began to give it to them. Then their eyes were opened and they recognized him, and he disappeared from their sight. They asked each other, "Were not our hearts burning while he talked with us on the road and opened the Scriptures to us?"
Luke 24:30-32 NIV

Then He said to Thomas, "Reach your finger here, and look at My hands; and reach your hand here, and put it into

My side. Do not be unbelieving, but believing."
John 20:27 NKJV

Jesus burns with desire to be with you. He desires it so much that He came to the earth, lived as a man and suffered the results of sin for you. He desired Thomas in **John 20:27** to believe that He appeared to Thomas and had him touch the holes in His hands and sides. Jesus burns for you to know Him. Will you take that step and know Him. Faith is an action.

"Before long, the world will not see me anymore, but you will see me. Because I live, you also will live. On that day you will realize that I am in my Father, and you are in me, and I am in you. Whoever has my commands and keeps them is the one who loves me. The one

*who loves me will be loved by my Father, and I too will love them and **show myself to them**."*
John 14:19-21 NIV (emphasis added)

But he who is joined to the Lord is one spirit with Him.
1 Corinthians 6:17 NKJV

The Encounter

*I have heard of You by the hearing of the ear,
But now my eye sees You.*
Job 42:5 NKJV

I can remember one of the first times I encountered Jesus face to face like it was yesterday.

I had been recently saved and I joined a missions organization by accident. I wanted to join a protestant ministry school that mimicked a monastic lifestyle where I could spend plenty of time one on one with God and also get some good teaching. I called one school and told them what I was looking for. They told me that's what their school was like. When I got there, it was not like a monastery at all. Most of my time was spent working and doing schoolwork. I Burned to spend time with Jesus and had to learn to rest in oneness with Him. I began to seek Jesus as I mowed the lawn, I would dance in worship while using the weed eater. I truly learned that Jesus would never leave us nor forsake us.

God said He will never leave us nor forsake us (Deuteronomy 31:6) and also that He is in us and we are in Him (John 15:5). So we can encounter Jesus Christ in everything we do.

Whenever I could I would still run to my dorm room and fall to my knees and worship and pray, seeking Jesus the best way I knew how. Then one day Jesus was standing physically in my room.

"How can I be your bride when I am so dirty?"

Jesus walked to my left side, knelt down, put His arm around me, embraced me, and said, "But I make you clean."

I broke down and cried my eyes out. That was one of the most beautiful encounters I have ever had with Jesus.

There is a transformation that happens inside of us when we realize that we are clean and Jesus has wiped all our sins away. When that lightbulb goes on, there is nothing that will hold us back from an intimate relationship with Jesus.

I have noticed that the greatest deception in the church is telling people, "You are a sinner." That statement causes people to look at themselves negatively and in turn build a false wall between them and Jesus. When we realize that we are clean and no longer have to live in sin, or sin ever again, we are totally set free and can focus on our relationship with Jesus. If we do slip up and sin, it's okay. We can simply repent and move on. Jesus loves us and wants us to be free and to know Him.

> *What shall we say then? Shall we continue in sin that grace may abound? Certainly not! How shall we who died to sin live any longer in it? Or do you not know that as many of us as were baptized into Christ Jesus were baptized into His death? Therefore we were buried with Him through baptism into death, just as Christ was raised from the dead by the glory of the Father, even so we also should walk in newness of life.*
> **Romans 6:1-4 NKJV**

God desires to encounter us, He desires to know us , and for us to enjoy His creations. He desires it so much that He made himself into an image to create you that you may be able to hang out with Him. It is His perfect will for you to be free and enjoy life! It is His perfect will for you to be with Him and for your family to be with Him! He desires it so much that He will do anything to get your attention. He will do anything for you to just realize you can know Him and be free! He wanted you to know Him so bad He humbled Himself and was born flesh of His own creation and suffered to pay the laws of the spirit concerning sin and death. He was wiped to the point of His internal organs being exposed so that you may be healed!

*Surely He has borne our griefs
And carried our sorrows;
Yet we esteemed Him stricken,
Smitten by God, and afflicted.
But He was wounded for our transgressions,
He was bruised for our iniquities;
The chastisement for our peace was upon Him,
And by His stripes we are healed.*
Isaiah 53:4-5 NKJV

Realize that love and realize your encounters.

It doesn't matter what your background is, how you got saved, or how much you know about the scriptures. The pivotal moment is now! God wants to hang out with you, He wants to know you so, let's hang out!

Desire and Your Heart

*Delight yourself also in the LORD,
And He shall give you the desires of your heart.*
Psalm 37:4 NKJV

Have you ever thought, "Why am I not getting to know God? I'm doing everything I can and I'm not getting closer to Him."

God took me through a process of getting rid of religious mindsets to enter into a relationship with Him. I was getting so fed up with not being able to communicate in a dialogue with Him. I wanted to know what God's favorite color is, His favorite flower, or what He thought about the shirt that I was wearing.

I didn't want to keep living without tangibly experiencing God.

I tried reaching out to people who looked like they knew God, and asking them for advice. One person was a well known preacher that traveled the world. At one of his meetings in Santa Cruz, CA, he was up front praying for people and I was excited to meet him. I thought, *Surely he can help me get to know God.*

I walked up to him and said, "Hey, thank you for your time. I need to know God. How can I really have a relationship with Him?"

The preacher replied, "Read the Psalms."

I walked away listless.

The next place I reached out to was a world-renowned ministry where people go to encounter God and get healed from sickness and emotional issues. I called their prayer hotline multiple times and one conversation went like this:

"Hi. How may I pray for you?"

"I need to know God. I honestly read, study, pray, and meditate more than anybody I know. How can I really know God?"

"Just keep doing what you're doing. Keep studying the Word and praying."

No one seemed to have answers for me.

Looking back I can see that that was the valley God was walking me through before I reached the mountain. I wanted more than visions, angelic encounters, signs, wonders, and miracles. I wanted God to walk with me in the Garden and show me the tree He created today. I wanted Him.

So what's the answer?..... BELIEF...

Belief is an action. Jesus told the Centurion in **Matthew 8:13 TNJB** ***"Go back, then; let this be done for you, as your faith demands."*** The action / faith of the Centurion demanded results. Jesus asked me concerning this scripture *"Do you not think he struggled in his thought as he rode out to meet me? Do you not think his men questioned his judgement and caused him to doubt? Yet he chose to have faith and keep riding, his action was faith and his action demanded."* With this in mind I have learned to choose to believe I have learned to expect to meet with Jesus when I seek Him, I have learned to expect Him to communicate with me when I talk with Him.

Jesus said to him, "If you can believe, all things are possible to him who believes." Immediately the father of the child cried out and said with tears, "Lord, I believe; help my unbelief!
Mark 9:23-24 NKJV

James 2:18 says I will show you my faith by my works. With that thought is it enuff you to have money in the bank and expect your groceries to show up or must you perform the act and use the money to buy groceries? I learned we must really put our belief into action. So I started self talk and activated what I believed, for example we are one with God so that means he is never away from us there is no separating us. I would then begin to help myself realize God is here and then ask God how He is doing and what He thought about things or what He was doing today. The more I do this the more tangible He gets.

It is really that simple and you might say I do believe! Ok I don't doubt that, but let's look at some things GOD says about belief then I will walk us through some practices to really get to know GOD in the next section.

But without faith it is impossible to please Him, for he who comes to God must believe that He is, and that He is a rewarder of those who diligently seek Him.
Hebrew 11:6 NKJV

"And these signs will follow those who believe: In My name they will cast out demons; they will speak with new tongues; they will take up serpents; and if they drink anything deadly, it will by no means hurt them; they will lay hands on the sick, and they will recover."
Mark 16:17-18 NKJV

"Therefore I tell you, whatever you ask for in prayer, believe that you have received it, and it will be yours."
Mark 11:24 NIV

Why is desire so important and why does God talk about desire? The dictionary describes desire in the Verb context as "strongly wish for or want (something)" then in the noun context "a strong feeling of wanting to have something or wishing for something to happen." We understand from scripture that desire stems from the heart and when we feel love, anger, or worry we feel those emotions flowing/ radiating from our heart are a form of desire.

So let us look deeper into the subject.

> *Delight yourself in the Lord, and he will give you the desires of your heart.*
> ***Psalm 37:4 NKJV***

> *What the wicked dreads will come upon him, but the desire of the righteous will be granted.*
> ***Proverbs 10:24 NKJV***

> *You will seek me and find me, when you seek me with all your heart.*
> ***Jeremiah 29:13 NKJV***

Science has discovered that the heart is the primary thinker in our body, but not only that, the heart has a magnetic field that is 60x stronger than the mind. This magnetic field envelops every cell of the body and can be measured from a number of feet away. One person's heart signal can affect another's brainwaves, and that the heart-brain synchronization can occur between two people when they interact. It appears that as individuals increase psychophysiological coherence, they become more sensitive to the subtle electromagnetic signals communicated by those around them. Taken together, these results suggest that cardiac electromagnetic communication may be a little-known source of information exchange between people, and that this exchange is influenced by our emotions.

(Citation Heart Magnetic Field) http://www.information-book.com/biology-medicine/biofields-heart-electromagnetic-field/ https://www.heartmath.org/assets/uploads/2015/02/the-energetic-heart-gci-edition.pdf

So with this information what can the desires in our heart do for us when we learn to engage them? Since science says that our hearts electromagnetic fields envelop every cell of our body our whole being will fall into alignment, and since our hearts magnetic waves can affect another person's brain waves our kingdom standards that we hold will begin to manifest in the people's lives around us and they can begin to experience God, because of those magnetic waves coming off of us, and their thoughts will begin to change and have the thoughts of God, and live at a higher standard.

How do we engage Desire? What I have learned about God is that if you try your best and take a step out in faith He will step in and walk with you the rest of the way. All you gotta do is try your best. The way God showed me was when I was in worship and you know when you begin to feel the adoration, thankfulness, or love radiate from your heart and you begin to kind of focus on and allow those things to flow? In the same way He said I can engage desire in my heart and allow it to radiate out of my heart at all times and live from that place. So right there in worship I focused my attention on my heart and said "I engage desire." I then began to feel the energy of desire in my heart then proceeded to engage different areas of desire. The first being my desire for Jesus. Learning to bring my focus back to that place throughout the day is fun and a wonderful part of the journey. Also with this practice I began to engage the Lord's desire for my children and release His desires over my children.

IMAGINATION

*And the LORD said, Behold, the people are one, and they have all one language; and this they begin to do: and now nothing will be restrained from them, which they have **imagined** to do.*
Genesis 11:6 KJV (emphasis added)

*And they began to make bricks and burn fires to build the city and the tower that they had **imagined** to complete. And the building of the tower was unto them a transgression and a sin, and they began to build it, and whilst they were building against the Lord God of heaven, they **imagined** in their hearts to war against him and to ascend into heaven.*

Book of Jasher 9:24-25 (emphasis added)

Our imagination is powerful. In the Old Testament, before there were many languages, people tried to build a tower that reached into heaven, but God stopped them in their tracks. Is it even possible to build a tower into heaven? In the book of Genesis, God said it would be. And in the Book of Jasher (a non-canonical book) it says, "they **imagined** in their hearts to war against him and to **ascend into heaven**" (Book of Jasher 9:24-25, emphasis added).

Our imagination is a tool that we can use not only to build things on earth, but to ascend into heaven. How and why is that even possible? First let's look at what it means to be created in God's likeness.

Then God said, "Let us make mankind in our image, in our likeness, so that they may rule over the fish in the sea and the birds in the sky, over the livestock and all the wild animals, and over all the creatures that move along the ground."
Genesis 1:26 NIV

See what great love the Father has lavished on us, that we should be called children of God! And that is what we are! The reason the world does not know us is that it did not know him. Dear friends, now we are children of God, and what we will be has not yet been made known. But we know that when Christ appears, we shall be like him, for we shall see him as he is. All who have this hope in him purify themselves, just as he is pure.

1 John 3:1-3 NIV

The question of the day is, what is our imagination? How do we go about planning a project or cooking a meal? We use our imagination. Our imagination is triggered consciously and subconsciously by the desire in our heart.

For instance, when you are about to crack an egg to begin frying it, what do you do? You picture/ imagine where you are going to crack the egg. When it's time to flip the egg, your imagination is at work showing you how to flip the egg with a spatula.

Even as you are reading this book, you are imagining different scenarios I'm telling you about.

I would like to play with the idea that our imagination is an operating system that can literally create what we desire.

> *"It is written in the prophets, 'And they shall all be taught by God.' Therefore everyone who has heard and learned from the Father comes to Me."*
> **John 6:45 NKJV**

When I was attending ministry school, I sat in my room pondering the things of God and how the Holy Spirit could teach me spiritual things. One day I was by myself outside of a friend's house and I asked the Holy Spirit to teach me. I saw multiple curtains or veils in front of me separating dimensions in the atmosphere. Then I stepped through the veils into realms of God.

I perceived the first veil as the curtain that was torn from top to bottom at the crucifixion of Jesus that separated the Holy of Holies from the inner court in the temple. I stepped through the torn veil into the Holy of Holies and stood in the presence of Jesus. I enjoyed simply gazing at Him looking into His eyes, examining His form and receiving His being. When in His presence the possibilities are endless.

Something fun you can do is to ask Jesus to take you wherever He wants you to go. A few times He took me to outer space and we sat in the middle of the stars. Sometimes when I go places with Him, He will speak to me, and other times we enjoy each other's company without saying anything.

Why don't you try it? I also suggest recording your encounters whether it be written, audio, or video. It is great to be able to go back and look at what Jesus has done.

Go somewhere where you won't be disturbed for at least 15 minutes.

Read through the steps below, and then go for it.

1. In your imagination, picture a school bus. When you can see the school bus, imagine it to be purple.

2. Now in the same way, picture Jesus.

3. In your imagination, walk up to Jesus and give Him a hug.

4. Ask Jesus to take you somewhere and show you something.

Here is another exercise you can do after you are comfortable with the first one.

1. Stand up someplace where you have room to step forward and backward.

2. Picture an open doorway in front of you.

3. Take one step forward through the doorway (physically and also in your imagination) into the presence of Jesus.

4. See yourself standing in front of Jesus.

5. Hang out with Jesus. You can talk with Him, listen to Him, or do an activity with Him.

6. When you're done, step backward slowly through the door (physically and in your

imagination) into the earth.

These are two exercises to catapult you in your relationship with God. Have fun!

Veil: Body, Soul, and Spirit

Now may the God of peace Himself sanctify you completely; and may your whole spirit, soul, and body be preserved blameless at the coming of our Lord Jesus Christ.
1 Thessalonians 5:23 NKJV

Even to this day when Moses is read, a veil covers their hearts.
2 Corinthians 3:15 NIV

Behold, I stand at the door and knock. If anyone hears My voice and opens the door, I will come in to him and dine with him, and he with Me.
Revelation 3:20 NKJV

God wants us to know Him more than anything. He wants us to walk with Him, to touch Him, to see Him, to even recognize the sound of Him walking when He comes to hang out with us in the cool of the day, like He did with Adam and Eve.

The apostle Paul said, "He is the image of the invisible God, the firstborn over all creation" (Colossians 1:15 NKJV).

God wanted us to be with Him so bad that He made Himself into an image, Jesus, so that He could make us into that image, and be able to have a relationship with us.

Think about that. He made Himself into an image to be able to create you in that image and be with you.

Now get this. When Adam and Eve fell and turned from God, He did everything possible to bring us back into relationship by choosing to suffer and die for us. God is good!

****

One day as I was pondering this Scripture, God revealed something to me about how He made humans.

For the word of God is living and powerful, and sharper than any two-edged sword, piercing even to the division of soul and spirit, and of joints and marrow, and is a discerner of the thoughts and intents of the heart.
Hebrews 4:12 NKJV

God showed me the separations of our being between the body, soul, and spirit. I could feel my soul and how different it felt from my spirit, like oil and water. I believe it is important to know the different realms of our being to better operate with them and to also help renew ourselves into that being we were created to be. With that said, I would like to give you my revelation on the difference between our body, soul, and spirit.

There are different veils or areas of our body, soul, and spirit, as well as a large veil that holds the different areas of our being. The best analogy I can use is a glass jar filled with water and oil. As they settle in the glass, they separate.

Let's say the glass is our body, the oil is our soul, and the water is our spirit. Oil and water are liquid, yet they don't mix in the same glass because they are different weights and substances. They seem to have some kind of veil of separation that holds them.

That is the way I see our spirit and soul in our body. There is something that keeps them separate, but also allows them to interact with each other.

Above everything else, our focus should be on getting to know Jesus, surrendering to His will for us, and allowing Him to flow through our being and clean us out. One of my daily prayers is, "Jesus, help me to go deeper in my relationship with you today and know you better than I did yesterday. Holy Spirit, please don't leave me the same today as I was yesterday."

As I pray that prayer, the Holy Spirit regularly shows me ungodly attitudes and actions that hinder me from seeing Jesus more clearly. These things sit in the veils between the different parts of my being and need to be cleared out so that I can know Him more.

One example is my frustration. Sometimes I would be frustrated with my children because they wouldn't listen to me. I thought, *Why don't they listen to me? After everything I do for them, can't they simply be quiet when the baby is sleeping?* That thought was sitting in my imagination, which is part of my soul.

God spoke to me and said, "What if I said that to you?" I thought about it and told Him, "That would be selfish because you are God and able to do anything. I'm still working on becoming perfect like you." Then I understood what He was trying to tell me about my attitude toward children. My thoughts were self-centered. This verse came to mind.

Let nothing be done through selfish ambition or conceit, but in lowliness of mind let each esteem others better than himself.
Philippians 2:3 NKJV

By cleaning out my stinking thinking, I was able to better love my family and more clearly look upon Jesus.

Now, let's look at the different veils in our being that we can walk through and engage our Lord Jesus. Think about our body. How many physical senses do we have? At a minimum, we have five senses including touch, taste, hearing, sight, and smell. I'll give you an example of touch. When I was younger I used to smoke and I really enjoyed it. When I quit, sometimes I would still feel a cigarette in my hand. My fingers wanted to handle a cigarette. That area of my body wasn't fully cleared of that addiction and wasn't having the presence of Jesus fully flowing through it.

Now let's think about our soul. How many areas exist in our soul? The basic areas are our imagination, conscious thoughts, subconscious thoughts, emotions, choice, and will. As we already described, our imagination is powerful and it needs cleansing, like every other part of our being. The

Bible tells us to think upon these things.

> *Finally, brethren, whatever things are true, whatever things are noble, whatever things are just, whatever things are pure, whatever things are lovely, whatever things are of good report, if there is any virtue and if there is anything praiseworthy—meditate on these things.*
> **Philippians 4:8 NKJV**

I've felt a huge shift in the presence of Jesus in my life by changing the way I think. When I think about Jesus and His goodness, I can begin to feel His presence all over my body. So by cleaning this area of our soul, the kingdom begins to flow more through us.

How about your spirit? What areas does your spirit have? This one is a little tricky, so let's think about what helps us to engage with God. How about things like worship, faith, hope, intuition, prayer, reverence, and fear of God. I don't believe these areas necessarily have to be cleansed, but I do believe they need to be developed.

When all the areas of your body, soul, and spirit are cleansed and flowing, there will be a huge shift in you, your household, and neighborhood, because nothing will be stopping the flow. It does take effort, but everything worthwhile does. What I like to do before moving forward is to worship Jesus and make sure my focus is on Him even if it's just 5 minutes. Let's just express our whole being to Him and thank Him for being good, for being real, for loving us so much and having so much more for us.

Spirit

The veil we learned to walk through in the last chapter was the veil of the spirit, and that is a great place to start. To take it a little further and engage your spirit, do the following:

- Close your eyes and place your right hand on your diaphragm and your left hand on top of your right.

- Move your right hand an inch from your body then put it back on your diaphragm.

- This time imagine moving your right hand in the same way, but don't move it. Move your spirit right hand out of your body, then your left. Step your right leg out, then your left, so that your spirit is standing in front of your body.

- With your spirit grab the veil and step through into the presence of God.

This practice takes engaging heaven to another level.

Soul
The veil of the soul is the darkness you see when you close your eyes. When you close your eyes envision yourself stepping into that darkness and standing in it. When you are there you can engage the Holy Spirit and He does some awesome things. Also you

can step through the veil there into the presence of God. Then when you are comfortable the same way when you stepped out of your body then through the veil step through the veil of your soul the same way. One time I stepped into the darkness when you closed your eyes. I stood there and welcomed the Holy Spirit to manifest Himself. The Holy Spirit then flies around me wrapping Himself around me and says I am always with you. I then see the heavenly angels all around me as well. One thing I like to do when engaging the soul I like to ask Jesus for His mind, also I receive His atmosphere, and glory and bring those things back through the veil into my soul and release them. I feel a great shift in my being when doing this. I also like to do this in all four areas of spirit, soul, body, and earth.

Body

The veil of the body is in your heart.

- What I do is I put my complete focus/ attention on my heart

- Then in my imagination I envision myself standing in my heart.

- Once my focus is there and I see myself standing there in my heart whatever it looks like

- I proceed to stand before the veil and step through forward

- I receive the atmosphere of Jesus

- Then I step backwards through the veil

- Continue as long as you like

A cool experience I had when I first began was stepping through the veil in my heart and standing before Jesus. He said, "Receive the blessings of your generations." I had different visions of my family bloodlines and receiving the blessings from each bloodline. I am half American Indian from both my mother and father. I saw a vision of a young native man standing in a field of wheat that was waist high. He was brushing his hand across the top of the wheat. I felt such love for creation flowing from him. As I received the blessings from my bloodlines, I got rocked by the goodness of Jesus!

****

A revelation God has shown me is that when we learn to engage the kingdom and allow Jesus to flow through the veils in the different areas in our being, there will eventually be a continuous flow and we will release the kingdom everywhere we go. In the Kingdom I have never encountered anxiety, so when we are around people the atmosphere of the Kingdom can be released and people can begin to relax and be able to really experience Jesus. For example, from my resting in God's presence and allowing Him to flow through my being people have told me that when I am around them or even walk into the room they feel like everything is going to be alright and everything is going to be taken care of. From the atmosphere of the Kingdom the person can relax and it allows their being to be less guarded and in turn begin to experience Jesus. A little more sentence example is, one time I woke up and everything was black and white like a sheer curtain over the color of the world. As I went about my day I would see Jesus standing behind me in my mind and He would manifest the thoughts 'Jesus has paid for it all' and I would see myself fall back into His arms. At that very moment I would feel the glory of God being poured over me from the top of my head to the souls of my feet and it was like a cold water hose on the hottest summer day in that I could feel the glory touching every cell of my body. This would happen a handful of times a day for three days. The Kingdom began manifesting so much that I would walk into a room and people would become heavily medicated they would heavily relax and lay back. On one account my friend

I was on a train going into the city and there was a woman who was possessed with lust and I could see in the spirit the demon was wanting to kill me. So in the spirit I grabbed the demon and through it into hell I then exploded my spiritman into light and filled the train with the light and made it a demon free zone. It was wonderful to see everyone free from any type of demonic influence. Everyone was way more at peace and was able to relax. If any of you have been to Boston and have ridden the subways, peace and relaxation is a rare event for most people there.

The Kingdom and God the Father, Son, and Holy Spirit are so much different than we can imagine. The deeper we go, the more we realize there is so much more to experience. When we spend time with Jesus getting to know Him His kingdom and who He is will begin to manifest in our lives and He is able to literally lavish His love on us. It's a wild ride and a lot of fun.

YOU ARE A SON

Behold, what manner of love the Father hath bestowed upon us, that we should be called the sons of God: therefore the world knoweth us not, because it knew him not.
1 John 3:1 NKJV

Never limit yourself, you were created in the image and likeness of God Himself! You are the image of God and able to do the same works as God. Our Lord Jesus said *"Most assuredly, I say to you, he who believes in Me, the works that I do he will do also; and greater works than these he will do, because I go to My Father. John 14:12 NKJV*

One thing that really saddens me Is when I hear believers limiting themselves. I hear believers say so often I am a feeler, I am a seer, I don't really feel things, but I see them. To broaden our understanding and to understand where I am coming from. How many senses do you have? Touch, taste, smell, sight, and hearing right? How long have you been using them? You have a pretty good handle on them right? Well, when you are born you have to learn to use those senses and the operations of those senses. It is the same in the spirit you have senses and have to learn how to use them you have to learn their operations. You don't say to your baby he/she is a seer because they can see but don't respond to your voice or touch right? That is such a limitation on your baby, on you, and the body of Christ! It is a limitation on who you are! If you do operate in a specific area more than another area, don't limit yourself or believe you are that, instead say I can operate stronger in this area right now, but am learning how to operate in the other senses.

People place these senses on their destiny they place them on who they are. They believe just because they can see in the spirit they are a prophet or because they can go on the streets and preach or heal the sick that they are an evangelist. In those specific offices of the five fold ministries it is a specific mantle that is placed on those individuals. If one desires a focus, a focus on what to be, then focus on being a son and getting to know Jesus. That is a gift that has been released upon all of us, a blessing beyond what our minds can fully comprehend at this very moment.

But as many as received him, to them gave he power to become the sons of

God, even to them that believe on his name:
John 1:12 NKJV

Praise be to the God and Father of our Lord Jesus Christ, who has blessed us in the heavenly realms with every spiritual blessing in Christ.
Ephesians 1:3 NKJV

What do you see here? From these scriptures and the ones you can recall in your mind what do you see? Who are you? Who were you created to be? How important are you?

How important are you? GOD the uncreated one made Himself into an image to be able to create you in that image just to be able you hang out with you! Man! You are special!

Who were you created to be? I think John the beloved sums it up best.

> *Behold, what manner of love the Father hath bestowed upon us, that we should be called the sons of God: therefore the world knoweth us not, because it knew him not.*
> ***1 John 3:1 NKJV***

So let me ask again… What do you see here? Who are you? Why were you created?

He loves you.

Testimonies

And they overcame him by the blood of the Lamb and by the word of their testimony, and they did not love their lives to the death.
Revelation 12:11 NKJV

I believe when we share testimonies it releases an atmosphere for the person hearing it to operate in the same encounter. So I would like to share a few testimonies of my own face-to-face encounters with Jesus and of others who I have led into encounters.

- I was 17 when I first encountered Jesus but before then my whole life I could not see or hear the name Jesus. People would try and lead me to the Lord Jesus, but I could not hear them nor could I really pay attention. So my first encounter with the Lord Jesus was at a Church Camp. It was a Holy Roller Penicastal Church Camp where people were really getting touched by God. They were running around, shouting in tongues, people getting slain in the spirit, and going into different encounters. I was just sitting there not knowing what was going on. Then all of a sudden God Himself reached into me and pulled every form of wickedness from me. Then everything turned white, but different shades of white, then a good brother listened to God and sat next to me and asked if I would like to pray and receive Jesus. For the first time in my life I said YES!

- I began to read and pray all day and night. I would literally spend all day and night reading and praying I wanted to know all that

I could. So one night I am on my knees praying and focusing on Jesus. When all of a sudden I see the face of Jesus moving toward me with His hands by His cheeks. A couple days later I am awakened by something putting their hand on my chest like they are leaning down to kiss my face. I then woke up and said to myself "someone tried to kiss me." I then rolled over to my side with my eyes closed only to open them staring at a being all blue like the face of Jesus I saw a few days prior. As I looked at this being that was blue but transparent I could see through the walls that were on the other side of Him. This being then turned and looked at me and when they did I freaked out and fainted.

- Some time passed by and I ended up turning from God and refused to listen to anything He would tell me. As soon as I would hear the voice of God telling me something I would shut it down and say NO! So one day I am at my friend's house and he goes to sleep in his room and I go to the living room to watch some T.V. As I sit on his couch the Holy Spirit says to me "Read you Bible" I say no I rather watch t.v. then The Holy Spirit says again "Read your Bible" and I give in and say fine. I grab my Bible and just open it. It opens to Mathew

25 the story about the talents. The Holy spirit begins to teach me inner audibly with His voice and then in my heart with the language of the spirit. You see each word depending on how you say it has a different feeling to it. For example say 'THE' now say 'LOVE' say that you love someone like your child or spouse. Now say you love and object. What do you feel when you say those things? Each has a different feeling to them. So The Holy Spirit was teaching me like this about the talents and HE did it three times. Each time He did it he made it hurt extremely badly so I would never forget it and after each time I said wow! I was really enjoying it. Then He spoke

to me outer audibly. His voice was so strong and powerful it threw me back against the couch and was squishing me against the couch. I began to shake like I was having a seizure and He said **"THIS IS MY VOICE AND YOU WILL LISTEN"** I said "ok" and it stopped. From that point I realized that the world has nothing to offer me but hurt and death. I have nowhere to go , but GOD. Ths being who I had no desire to know or go after HE came after me! I needed to know this being! So I then spent as much time as I could seeking God the best way I know and God showed up. I started just laying down and putting all my focus on Jesus and I would be taken to different places with the Lord Jesus. A few times he would take me to outer space and we would walk on these clouds that were purple and white. I would walk down the clouds and He Jesus would be standing there waiting for me. It is such a privilege to be able to see and get to know God. And it's for everyone! We were all created in His image, so that we can know Him.

- I wanted more, I desired more than these encounters, even now I need more, I wanted to conversate with Jesus to know what he was processing at the moment to really have a relationship with our Lord. It burned so intensely it was to the point where I leave my body and come to you or you come to me. I would spend around 12hrs a day sometimes more seeking Jesus. Having wonderful encounters going to different places in the world and releasing Heaven. One time while I was in L.A. I was worshiping and praying in my hotel room and a physical portal opened up in front of me, so I decided I would step through. A dragon physically touched me and pushed me back through into my hotel room. I said "Heck No!" I forced my way through and ended up in outer space. I say all kinds of constellations which I couldn't tell you what they are, for the only constellations I know are the common ones. Then inside the constellations I saw dragons embedded I then proceeded to ask the Lord what am I to do? He then handed me a scroll. I then asked the Lord Jesus again what am I to do with the scroll. He then had me blow through it like a fiddle and the dragons were removed and cast elsewhere to hell. He then released heavenly being into the constellation.

- One occasion I was in Redwood City California visiting family and I needed some time to meditate. So I went to the library after my meditation. I needed to use the facilities. While washing my hands there was a homeless individual grooming himself. I asked the Lord Jesus for a word for him that he may experience God. I heard nothing so I left. As I was walking out the door I said to the Lord "No, you have something for him" I walked back in and stood next to the man. Not knowing what to say and being immature I asked him "So are you homeless?" Trying to strike up a conversation. We end up going out to the picnic tables to chat. At the end of our conversation I ask him if he would like to see Jesus? He in turn said yes. I led him to the Lord Jesus and after I told him I have been saving some money to give away and it was all I had and I would like to give it to him. I pull out the money being $1.63 he receives it gladly then he pulls out his wallet and opens it up being packed with big bills. He pulls out $60 AND GIVES IT TO ME.

- One evening I was reading my bible on the couch at my uncle B's and Aunty Colleen's house. Then all of a sudden the intense presence of Jesus physically came into the room and I could see Him, but transparent like a heat mirage. And He walked in front of me then sat next to me and read the bible with me.

- I used to go on these ministry trips to the homeless in S.F. and we would walk in teams around the city chatting with people and handing out supplies as needed. There was one individual that I remember leading to Jesus he got really touched and I will not forget him. We were on the sidewalk at night in the city. I asked him if he would like to see Jesus. So I led him through the process and he deeply encountered Jesus and the intense presence of our Lord Jesus filled the area and the gentleman began to weep with the Lord Jesus.

- When two of my cousins were around 7 years old I asked then if they would like to see Jesus. Sure they replied. I led them through the encounter to Jesus both of their faces shined like a flashlight was pointed at their face. One said that Jesus took her and showed her how the pyramids were made. The other said Jesus took him to outer space. The next day one of them started to operate in the manifestation of heaven in the natural realm around her and was telling me she began to see animals running around and flying around her. I told her it's normal and I do as well experience the same.

- One morning I came home from working overnight and layed in bed wanting to spend some time with Jesus before trying to get a couple hours of sleep before school. I was laying on my face just telling Jesus I love Him then in a vision I saw Jesus as a father and I grabbed Him gave Him the biggest hug and He embraced me. Then He started tickling me and I could physically feel His fingers tickling my ribs. It was one of the most wonderful encounters I had.

- I used to work overnight in a retirement home "assisted living" and there was a gentleman that was a Missionary for the

Mormon Church. He was on my rounds and we used to talk of the Lord Jesus and it was great I really miss our talks. One night I asked Him if he would like to see Jesus. Of course he said. I told Him how about right now? So I led him into the encounter with Jesus and this gentleman was really encountering the Lord Jesus. I told him to walk up to the Lord and give Him a hug and he physically moves his arms to give a hug. I then ask him to ask Jesus to take him somewhere and he moves his arms to open a door and is gone in a trance, so I just sneak away and let him enjoy his time.

- The was a young man at a fast food restaurant in Manteca California. A friend and I began a conversation with him and he was telling me what things he believed. I asked The Holy Spirit what He would like me to do and he gave me a vision of me putting my hand on his chest and the other on his back. I in turn asked the young man "Do you wanna feel something?" Sure he said what are you going to do? I then put my hands where I saw God tell me. One his chest and back. Then the young man starts tilting backwards and saying whoooo. I take my hands off him but keep then pointed in the same direction. At his chest and back. I tell him "I am not touching you its not me it's God" he then falls on the ground and loudly saying "I cant get up I have sticky cups all over my body" I walk to the side of him, bend down next to him and say "Do you believe now?" "Yes I believe yes I believe!" The young man loudly proclaims. About 10 minutes later my friend and I see the young man walking around and talking to someone but we can't see anyone. The young man has his wrist out like someone is guiding him. He then walks to us and tells us he can see Jesus and Jesus is leading him around.

Final Thoughts

You will meet people who will be against this concept that you can have a real relationship with Jesus. Not everyone will grasp it right now, but they will at some point. Just keep moving forward, because your life will show then it is possible. The Lord Jesus says in **Matthew 7:23 And then I will declare to them, 'I never knew you; depart from Me, you who practice lawlessness!** He says I never knew you. Meaning it is possible to know Him. He wants you to know Him. Lord Jesus also works with you in the process. If you step out He steps in. So just do your best when seeking to know Him and see Him. He will help you 100 percent. You will also notice at times that after a while he will step back for you to engage on your own so you can know a deeper understanding and also know how to activate that area or gift in your spirit. An example is one time I asked my children what is a story in the bible that you would like to go and visit with Jesus. My boy said the one where Jesus puts the guy's ear back on. My other boy said he wanted to go inside the necklace cross he got in the mail. We went on our journeys and as I was trying to find the garden of gethsemane I kept seeing Jesus put my younger boys cross on me. I kept that experience and sought later what the Lord was saying, But I was trying to see the garden. So I activated my imagination and pushed through and tried to picture what the garden was and it appeared.

I then saw on one knee picking up the ear Jesus was so full of love and compassion for this soldier. I also felt His love and willingness to go down this path the path of the cross. Then I looked and saw Peter standing there experiencing the love of Jesus for the soldier radiating off of Jesus. I also felt Peter's confusion , because the Lord Jesus told him to buy the sword.

In that experience I had you learn to use the tool God has given me a little more on my own to be able to engage that scene in His-tory.

"But without faith it is impossible to please him: for he that cometh to God must believe that he is, and that he is a

rewarder of them that diligently seek him."
Hebrews 11:6 NKJV

But he who is joined to the Lord is one spirit with Him.
1 Corinthians 6:17 NKJV

When you received Jesus as your Lord and Savior He made you and Him One spirit. You and God are literally one. So there is no longer a seeking God, for you and Him are one there is no separating you you have Him and He has you, but now it is a seeking to know Him.

In Hebrews the they interpreted a greek word for the statement "***of them that diligently seek him***" and that word is **ekzētéō** ἐκζητέω ekzētéō, ek-zay-teh'-o; from ἐκ and zētéō; to search out, i.e. (figuratively)investigate, crave, demand, (by Hebraism) worship:— en- (re-)quire, seek after (carefully, diligently).

This word has depth and also can express the feeling or desire behind it. Number one is that if you desire God and desire to know Him you will be rewarded. If you worship Him you will encounter Him. He will reward you at any place in life you are at.

I see a young woman sitting at her computer contemplating if she should write her book. Go for it the Lord Jesus will write through you and bless you. I see orange on you the wisdom of God.

I know when some people start to operate in different areas of the spirit that it is easy to want to make a ministry of it. If that is what the Lord has called you to then that is awesome just be sure to check yourself and see if your focus is leaving your family, for your primary focus should be your family. If anything starts to get in the way of family you need to rethink, replan, and adjust your schedule, for family is number one. If you look at all the problems in the world they all boil down to family being the root issue. Family is your first ministry as well. If you can't manifest the kingdom in your family what makes you think you're going to manifest it in the world? Transform your family, then transform your neighborhood, then your city, and so on.

One testimony from a person I know that has really stuck in my and has changed my life. This brother was taken to a room that has all the mantles of all the saints Jesus then tells Him to pick any mantle he would like. Some of the mantles are huge and so bright. In the far corner He saw a very small mantle, but it was brighter than all the other mantles. Jesus then tells him its Enoch's mantle then says why doesn't anyone just want to be known for knowing me?

I don't even care if I am known, nothing else in this world matters to me I just want to know Jesus. Paul says

casting down arguments and every high thing that exalts itself against the knowledge of God, bringing every thought into captivity to the obedience of Christ,
2 Corinthians 10:5 NKJV

Yet indeed I also count all things loss for the excellence of the knowledge of Christ Jesus my Lord, for whom I have suffered the loss of all things, and count them as rubbish, that I may gain Christ
Philippians 3:8 NKJV

I hope you are truly blessed and encouraged to know Jesus even more and realize how much He truly wants to know you. There is no longer a seeking for Him you have Him you and Him are one! Close your eyes and look at Him, walk to Him and hug Him you got Him and He has you!

Made in the USA
Columbia, SC
27 June 2025

59916685R00061